Poetry
Family
& Friends

By

Nancy E. Hutcherson

*** Forever Yours ***

Dear Lord, I thank you for my life and all you've given me,
My home, my family and my friends are all I ever need...
But you have given so much more that words cannot describe.
The peace, the love, the happiness that money cannot buy...

Oh Lord, I am forever Yours, please show me what to do,
And keep me close, don't let me stray,
My Life I Live For YOU...

Written by: Nancy E. Hutcherson
August, 2001

September 11, 2001

I walked outside this morning and viewed the sky above,
I asked the Lord why tragedy, why can't we live in love…
And then it came upon me, the answer plain and clear,
These are the times we call on God and hold our loved ones near.

When times are good we go along and do our daily thing,
We don't take time to say hello to someone who's in pain…
But let our nation under God be hit by Satan's hand,
We rally to each other every woman, child and man…

Why can't we change our attitudes towards one another now,..
And live each day with Love and Hope and show the world just how..
It shouldn't take a tragedy for us to live in Love,
We only have to keep our eyes on Jesus up above…

So let us stand upon this ground and let the whole world know,
We will not be defeated for our Lord is in Control…
We will change our attitudes toward one another now,
And live each day with love and hope and show the world just how…

Written by: Nancy E. Hutcherson
September 18, 2001

JESUS' NAME

How often do we talk to God or pray in Jesus' name,
And thank Him for the gifts we have instead of giving blame...

He's blessed us with so many gifts and walks with us each day,
He's never once left us alone not even when we stray...

And yet we fear to say His name, what is the reason why,
Is it because we listen to Satan and his lies...

Jesus died upon the cross for your sins and for mine,
How can we not proclaim Him as our Savior in these times...

I'm sorry that I've not stood up and said my Savior's name,
And given Him the credit instead of giving blame...

I've ended prayers "In His name I pray," so I would not offend,
Oh Jesus please forgive me, I won't do it again...

I stand here now in front of God and everyone I know,
Jesus is my Lord, my life and I never will let go...

Written by: Nancy E. Hutcherson
September 30, 2001

*** Take Control ***

My mind is in a whirlwind, you know the kind I mean…
Where everything goes round and round,
I feel like I could scream…

I'm rushing here and rushing there, I don't take time to stop,
And by the time my day is through,
I think my head will pop…

I cannot do this one more day, the stress is killing me…
I want to be a child again,
Where life is worry free…

Oh Lord, I know I am Your child, please take my cares away…
I want my life in Your control
I give you me today…

I'm kneeling right here where I am and asking from my heart…
I know I've strayed, I'm coming home,
Please show me how to start…

I feel my cares and fears subside, no longer feeling pain…
Your Son has come into my life,
I am Your child again.

Written by: Nancy E. Hutcherson
October 3, 2001

Rock of Jesus Christ

I will not live in fear my man,
Tis by the hand of God I stand,
My faith is on the rock of Jesus Christ...

I will not look in Satan's eyes,
He's only good at telling lies,
Twas Jesus, Son of God who paid the price...

Stand tall with me in God we trust,
The evil one cannot hurt us,
We have the Word of God on which to hold...

Join hands dear friends and let us pray,
Our Lord above will show the way,
We'll follow Him as in the days of old...

Written by: Nancy E. Hutcherson
October 4, 2001

*** Prayer ***

A prayer is something simple, it's just talking to our God,
Whether Church or home or work even driving in the car...
He always wants to hear from us, in good times and in bad,
When we don't pray or talk to Him, it makes Him really sad...

Some people say they just don't know, how to pray a prayer,
They think that God is far away and doesn't really care...
But let me tell you He does care, for each and every one,
That is why we have the Cross and He gave up His Son...

It's really something awesome to know that Jesus died,
Upon that cross for you and me so we could live our lives...
In truth and love and happiness and all the world could know,
Our sins are all forgiven by our God, who loves us so...

So give yourself a moment, it's easy when you start,
Just ask our Lord in Heaven to put Jesus in your heart...
He never will deny you for His love is always true,
A small prayer prayed just where you are is all you have to do...

Welcome to the family of Jesus Christ,

Written by: Nancy E. Hutcherson
October, 2001

*** *Guardian Angels* ***

Have you ever seen your angel with wings so snowy white,
Guarding you in daytime and protecting you at night...
They're always there around you no matter what you do,
You may not even know it, but they're watching over you...

God gave to us these angels to guide us through each day,
So if you want your Angels help, you only need to pray...
They do not take the place of God, they are only here to help,
There're always times we need them, I've called on them myself...

Some people say that they're not real, it's just a story line,
But I am here to tell you, that I've called mine many times...
They will not interfere with life if you don't ask them to,
They'll just be there in case you call, no matter what you do...

It tells us in the Bible that Angels are heaven sent,
You too will know, when Jesus calls, and then you will repent...
For God just wants His children to have the best of life,
So His angels are watching over us, both daytime and at night...

Just talk now to your angels, for they would love to hear,
You call upon them for their help, remember, they're always near...
And some day you may see one, floating high up in the sky,
And when you do, you will believe, they're always by your side...

Written by: Nancy E. Hutcherson
October 20, 2001

*** *Salvation* ***

Be it known to all who hear that Satan is alive,
Roaming freely on this earth and telling all his lies...
He started in the Garden where he tempted Eve,
She disobeyed the word of God and that's why Satan's free...

God didn't want His children to live apart from Him,
And so He brought His Son to bear our grief and all our sins...
Jesus came in human form upon this earth to teach,
Each and everyone of us that God's not out of reach...

H gave His life for one and all, high upon the Cross,
He did it cause He loved us, not wanting one soul lost...
But Satan's here to take away what Jesus did back then,
He tries to fill our hearts with hate and have us live in sin...

We do not have to listen, we have armor to put on,
The word of God is all we need and Satan must be gone...
He cannot hold us captive when God is on our side,
Command the evil one to leave and take with him his lies...

Please accept what Jesus did then you won't live apart,
From God and all His blessing, it's the only way to start...
And then you ask forgiveness for all your sins of past,
Now you've become a Christian, you're a child of Gods at last...

Written By: Nancy E. Hutcherson
October, 2001

*** *A DREAM* ***

I had a dream the other night, an angel came to me,
She took me by my hand and said,
There's something you should see…

We walked upon a golden street, the houses made of stones,
They were diamonds, emeralds and rubies,
She said this is your home…

We entered one so lovely, I could not believe my eyes,
I felt such love and happiness,
Coming from inside…

I saw some friends and family, that died in years of past,
They were so happy being there,
I wanted this time to last…

They took me to the garden, with streams of flowing wine,
The colors of the flowers,
Were something so divine…

Then upon a bolder, I saw Jesus sitting there,
A smile upon his handsome face,
The sun was in HIS hair…

He said, my child, I am so pleased,
But your life is not through,
For when it's time for you to leave,
Then I will come for you…

Written by: Nancy E. Hutcherson
Inspired by GOD
November 26, 2001

*** *HEY, GOD IT'S ME AGAIN* ***

Hey God, it's me again,
Calling out to you,
Asking for your help,
With a problem that is new...

I know you haven't heard from me,
In such a long, long time...
I've been doing things myself,
I didn't think you'd mind...

I wanted to be in control,
Of everything I do,
I didn't see any need,
Of calling upon you...

But God, it's just not working,
My life is in a mess...
Please take me back & hold my hand,
I really need to rest...

And God, if you would walk with me,
Each and every day...
I promise you, I won't forget,
To take the time to pray...

Written by: Nancy E. Hutcherson
December 1, 2001

*** *MONDAY'S PRAYER* ***

A new week is beginning,
And I have a chance to change...
Everything is now brand new,
And nothing is the same...

Everything that's in the past,
No longer exists for me...
My Lord has now forgiven,
And now I am set free...

I can be anything I want,
With help from God above...
I only have to live my life,
For Him and show His love...

So take my hand and let me show,
Just what He has in store...
He will change your life for you,
And give you so much more...

Written by: Nancy E. Hutcherson
December 1, 2001

*** *TEACHING CHILDREN* ***

Teaching children what to do,
Isn't very hard...
You only have to show them by your actions,
And your heart...

They always want to be like you,
In every way they can...
Monkey see, Monkey do,
That's what they understand...

No longer can you tell them,
Just do what I say...
You must always show them,
In the way you live each day...

So if you want your children,
To live their lives for God...
Then you must live your life that way,
It's really not too hard...

Written by: Nancy E. Hutcherson
December 1, 2001

Critter

Poems

By

Nancy E. Hutcherson

*** EVENING WITH CATS ***

I have 4 cats and a dog at home,
And it's safe to say that I'm never alone...
I take a bath and Frosty's there,
Dunking his paws and grooming his hair...

Here comes Holly she's prissy and sleek,
She circles Frosty, he slaps her cheek...
The water is running, the sprayer is on,
You'd think they'd be frightened and leave me alone...

But not these two, they are running this place,
Now here comes Cricket, she's entered their space...
They look at each other and fur starts to fly,
They're jumping on Cricket, I'm afraid she might die...

Then all of a sudden, they turn and they run,
My little OLE Cricket is having some fun...
She called their bluff with her hissing & spit,
Her back was hunched up, they decided to quit...

I'm out of the tub and heading for sleep,
And the 3 little critters want something to eat...
So I open the drawer and take out the can,
They gulp up the treats I hold in my hand...

I give them a squeeze and they give me a Mew,
And I know they are saying, "Hey Mom, we love you."

Written by: Nancy E. Hutcherson
October, 2001

Home Alone

I'm home alone, it's dark outside, the rain is pouring down,
I'm not afraid of man or beast, my critters are all around...
The trees are swaying greatly, the thunder makes a shout,
The lightning hit outside my door and took the electricity out...

Now you would think that Duke the Dog would guard my every
move,
But he's lying there asleep, there's nothing he will do...
I fumble for a flashlight in the table by the bed,
The Frost Man cat jumps up on me and landed on my head...

It scared me for a moment, I thought I'd been attacked,
Until I felt him curl up and his fur was on my back...
The lightning still was flashing and Miss Holly made the scene,
She flipped her tail at Frost Man and woke him from his dream...

He got his claw caught in the spread and Holly gave a howl,
Then Duke the Dog woke up as if to say, 'what is it now?'
I just cannot imagine what a scene we must have been,
A dog, two cats and me while the lightning still shines in...

I'm home alone this evening but I still am not afraid,
I have my little critters keeping all the spooks away...
You may think I'm crazy to feel safety here within,
But you don't know my critters, what a comfort they have been.

Written by: Nancy E. Hutcherson
October, 2001

Maggie & Duke

I looked outside my window, here comes Maggie up the road,
With Sandy, Mocha & Scooter following as she goes...
They're coming to see Duke Dog and gather in the yard,
They always stay around our road not straying very far...

Mocha sees Miss Chewy lying on the drive,
He thinks he'll have a little snack but Duke Dog comes alive...
He gets up off his pillow and bounds down to the walk,
He barks at Mr. Mocha and says we must have a talk...

You don't come near my Kitty for she's lived here for some time,
She's my friend and I'll protect her so you better get in line...
Miss Maggie prisses up the walk and nudges Duke Dog's head,
They kiss and then she turns around and gets on Duke Dog's bed...

Duke loves his little Maggie, she's his girlfriend that's a fact,
But he just can't keep up with her when she's lying in his sack...

Scooter always has a smile for everyone he meets,
He doesn't care what's going on, he only wants some treats...
These dogs are something special, they are a gift from God to us.
They'll guard our homes, they only want our love, some food &
trust...

Written by: Nancy E. Hutcherson
October 10, 2001

*** *Honey Bear* ***

I must tell you all a story, about the dog God brought to me,
Her name is Honey Bear, and she's as lovable as can be…
She has big eyes and creamy fur and her tail curls over her back,
She wiggles when you talk to her, personality she doesn't lack…

The day I brought her to our home, Big John was in the yard,
I was a little nervous, but she jumped right out of the car…
He asked me where did she come from, and I said she's just staying
awhile,
I'm sure I can find her another good home, then he looked at her
with a smile…

I told him her name is Honey Bear and he patted her on her head,
She wiggled her tail and licked his hand, then he asked if she'd been
fed…
I took her up into the house and she settled down on a towel,
Then Duke and the cats came out to see and she greeted them with a
howl…

Duke just looked, while Cricket ran then Frosty gave her a shrug,
But Holly the Princess walked over to her, and slowly she gave her a
rub…
I could hardly believe what I just saw, not a one started a fight,
They simply accepted this honey bear and they all settled in for the
night…

Now Honey Bear left us for a short while, to a home that wanted her
too,
And even though they all tried hard, she wanted to be back with
Duke…
Now she is back and I'm sure she'll stay cause she fits in with our
brood…
She just wants love and a pat on the head, and most of all lots of
food…

Written by: Nancy E. Hutcherson, October, 2001

*** Creatures ***

Some people think I'm quirky to like the things I do,
It's just that I love creatures and they seem to love me too…

There are many blue tailed lizards running up and down the walk,
I wouldn't think of killing one, they listen when I talk…

I also have some tree frogs that make a lot of noise,
They hop, they jump they try to hide, they are more fun than toys…

The bees are always buzzing round the flowers by the side,
They only want the nectar to take back to their hive…

The birds are something special as they dance up in the trees,
Just waiting for the feeder to be filled up with their seeds…

The butterflies are beautiful, their beauty can't compare,
And if I sit and do not move, they'll land upon my hair…

I can't forget the spiders, their webs they weave so fine,
They are such patient creatures, weaving webs takes lots of time…

God gave to us these creatures & many more for sure,
He asks us just to care for them, so all can long endure…

Written by: Nancy E. Hutcherson
October, 2001

*** *Squirrels* ***

Summer's gone and fall is here, it's time to gather food,
The squirrels are running here and there, they're being rather rude...
They do not join together to gather up the nuts,
They steel from one another and they really make a fuss...

I do so love to watch them, how they jump around the trees,
Sometimes they try to hide themselves by digging under leaves...
They jump and twirl and try to fly from the tree down to the fence,
They always seem to make it, I don't think they have much sense...

Then one just found the feeder that is hanging in the tree,
I fill it up for all the birds, so they will have some feed...
It's really quite amusing, to watch the squirrels survey,
The feeder and the squirrel proof door that keeps them all away...

They jump upon the feeder and hang there by their tails,
Just how they're doing what they are is really hard to tell...
Somehow they hit the lever and the seeds start falling down,
Now here come all the other squirrels, they're feasting off the
ground...

Some people do not like the squirrels, they think that they are pests,
But I am here to tell you that they're fun to watch no less...
God made these little critters just like He made the birds,
He gave them to us to care for, it's written in His word...

Written by: Nancy E. Hutcherson
October, 2001

*** *The Lizard* ***

I saw a baby lizard that fell in Duke Dog's bowl,
And if he doesn't make it out, He surely won't grow old…
I picked him up so gently, and put him on the ground,
Chewy cat saw what I did, and off the chair she bound…

I caught her quickly by her tail, of which she did not like,
I couldn't let her get to him, it would not be a fair fight…
She mewed at me as if to say, gosh, what have I done,
You always take my toys away, I never have much fun…

I watched the baby lizard, scurry under the chair,
I could not put my Chewy down, cause she saw he was there…
So I bent down to scoop him up, and Chewy wiggled free,
She gently bit me on my leg, and I fell down on my knees…

I guess we made a funny sight, lying on the ground,
When the mamma lizard just showed up, her baby had been found…
So I grabbed Chewy in my arms, to give them time to leave,
As mamma and her baby took off up the tree…

I love all of God's creatures, and they all deserve to live,
Each one has a purpose in this life for things to give…
The lizard is so special for it keeps the bugs away,
From our flowers and our gardens so they brighten up our days…

So when you see a Lizard
Playing in your yard…
Make sure you do not hurt him
Then he won't go very far.

Written by: Nancy E. Hutcherson
October 30, 2001

*** *26 Wild Turkeys* ***

I pulled into my driveway, to my home upon the hill,
And viewed a sight I'd not seen before and maybe never will...
26 wild turkeys were feeding in the yard,
I didn't want to frighten them and so I stopped the car...

I thought that I was dreaming, it was something to behold,
These 26 wild turkeys eating grass seed that was sowed...
They didn't seem afraid of me or mind that I was there,
They continued with their feeding as though they didn't care...

I wished I had my camera cause no one would believe,
These 26 fat turkeys just looking back at me...
I got out of the car so I could get a better look,
And the biggest and the fattest one came closer, then he shook...

It must have been a signal to the others so they'd know,
There was danger here, and it was time for them to go...
All at once they took to flight as I stood very still,
Watching 26 wild turkeys flying off my hill...

They've never come back to my yard but I know they're still around,
I can hear their gobbles in the woods, it's a very distinct sound...
If I had only had my camera, you would know this story's real,
26 wild turkeys eating seeds upon my hill...

Written by: Nancy E. Hutcherson
November 1, 2001

*** *Morris the Squirrel* ***

When I was just a little girl, playing outside in the fall,
I was watching a neighbor clean gutters, and my name he started to call…
I ran up to his ladder and he threw down a nest of leaves,
Baby squirrels were scurrying around, and I could hardly believe…

I was close to a wee little one, climbing the side of the house,
I grabbed him with my handkerchief, he felt like a furry mouse…
I took him home and asked my mom if I could keep him here,
She said, I guess that it's OK but he's small & may not live, dear…

I fed him with a doll bottle with milk that mom heated for me
He drank it and seemed to enjoy it, I was as happy as a little girl could be…
I named him Morris Jr., for that was the name of my dad,
They were the only boys in the house, a mother and sister I had…

Morris Jr. grew and he flourished, he ran free everywhere in our home,
Oh how I did love him, he was fun and I was never alone…
If he wanted to go outside, he would go to the door and climb up,
We would let him out for a short little while and then he came back to us…

He would eat with me at breakfast, he loved my toast and my eggs,
My chocolate milk he would suck up and then sat on his back legs…
He took his tail and wiped his mouth, I promise this is true,
You'd think that he had manners and was taught just what to do…

My little friend lived for some time and gave me lots of love,
I know that he was sent to me from Heaven up above…
But when he died, I cried and cried to lose one that's so dear,
But God above showed me His love my squirrel is always near…

Written by: Nancy E. Hutcherson
November 1, 2001

*** *The Horse* ***

I was cleaning up the kitchen when my husband yelled at me,
Come quickly to the window, there is something you must see...
I stopped what I was doing and yelled at him of course,
He said you won't believe it, but in the yard there is a horse...
Ever sense we built out here, strange things we see around,
Wild turkeys, foxes, chipmunks too, digging in the ground...
But never has there been a horse, for they just do not roam,
It must have gotten through a fence and strayed away from home...

I grabbed the leash I used for Duke and quietly left the house,
I used to have horses, so I was quiet as a mouse...
I realized I had no shoes, that was a stupid thing,
To try and catch a halter less horse in the open yard in the rain...
The horse was grazing on the grass and stopped and looked at me,
As if to say, what do you want, can't you see that I am free...
I didn't want him to get away and get down on the road,
The cars are always flying fast and speed is not controlled...

I walked up very slowly and was talking sweet and low,
I put the leash around his neck so I could have control...
He wasn't very happy and he raised his head up high,
He tried to free himself from me, my foot was by his side...
It only took a moment for his hoof to find my toes,
I tried to move my foot away and his chin hit my nose...
I did not turn him loose and I managed to hold on,
I did not want to lose him, I was afraid that he'd be gone...

He finally stopped his snorting and settled down a tad,
He let me walk him to the house, I was very glad...
I didn't let my husband know, my toes were killing me,
Or that my nose was really sore, I didn't want him to see...
He had called the neighbors and found the owner near,
She was coming for her horse and I was wishing she'd get here...
I was standing with the dog leash wrapped around his head,
She drove up with her trailer and this is what she said...

I just got this horse today and I took him to the barn,
I turned him lose in the pasture without his halter on…
I guess the fence is down somewhere, I'll check when we get home,
Thank you for the phone call, I must be getting on…

I went back in the house and laid down on the bed,
My toes and nose were hurting me and an ache was in my head…
Dear John, please clean the kitchen and then bring me a drink,
So I can lie here on the bed and think what I want to think…
I didn't worry anymore, I curled up with my kitties
As John closed the bedroom door.

Written by: Nancy E. Hutcherson
November 1, 2001

THE MOUSE IN THE HOUSE

There is a mouse within the house
I saw it yesterday......
Shasta and my Sassy cat
Wanted it to play....
They chased it in the kitchen
And tried to catch it there
Sassy doesn't have front claws
But Shasta doesn't care....
She jumped upon the counter
And was ready to attack...
Instead she watched the little mouse
Squeeze through a narrow crack...
She waited there in silence
Not making a move or sound
While Sassy crept around the frig
To see if the mouse was around...
Both cats stayed there for a long time
Waiting for the little thing
But it never did return that day
We'll see what tomorrow brings....

TOMORROW

Yesterday my kitties saw the mouse that's living here...
They tried their best to catch it but they could not get near...

It had many hiding places that the kitties did not know ...
The ones they knew were very small and they just could not go...

So they hid and they waited for the mouse to find the cheese...
That they had left in their food bowl
They were happy I could see...

27

This mouse was a very smart one
He knew what he should do...
He turned the water bowl over, grab the cheese and out he flew...

Now Sassy and Shasta are buddies
of that there is no doubt...
They like to chase each other all around the house...

Ever since they saw this little one
They wanted so to play...
They didn't want to hurt him
They just wanted him to stay...

They have become a little tired
From all the running round...
So they cuddled to each other and didn't make a sound...

The house was now so quiet
I almost fell asleep...
But then I saw that little mouse
Along the wall he creeped…

He snuck upon the kitties
Made a hole within their fur...
And he snuggled right between them
And no one said a word.....

Now the kitties had their playmate
He is different that is true...
But the mouse was very happy
For he had playmates too!

Written by: Nancy E. Hutcherson

*** *Tuffy the Cloud* ***

There is a cloud named Tuffy that lives up in the air,
He is such a little fellow, doesn't seem to have a care...
It's really fun to watch him as he scurries across the sky,
Changing from a little cloud to one that's twice his size...

Tuffy is a smart cloud, he can change the way he looks,
I've seen him as a dragon like you see in story books...
Sometimes he is an angel with wings so snowy white,
Ever changing as he goes, he makes a funny sight...

The best one that I ever saw, I thought it was a dream,
How on earth did Tuffy make the Christmas manger scene...
But I saw baby Jesus in the manger in the barn,
Then other clouds were gathering ever changing all their forms...

Joseph, mother Mary and some sheep were on the right,
Three wise men and a camel and a cow were next in sight...
Then there were all these shepherds standing here and there,
I could hardly believe, what I just saw up in the air...

So if you want to have some fun and see the things I do,
Just go outside and watch the clouds and Tuffy will show you...
All the different things he does and just what he can be,
You only have to watch him and then you must believe...

Written by: Nancy E. Hutcherson
November 2, 2001

*** *Tuffy The Cloud II* ***

Tuffy is that little cloud you see high in the sky,
He plays around from morn till night, he's always floating by...
He loves to entertain you with the changes that he makes,
He can be a teddy bear or a swan upon a lake...

It's so much fun to watch him when he plays with other clouds,
They bump into each other, it will make you laugh out loud...
Sometimes they form a circle and Tuffy's in the center,
He wants out so he can fly, so he makes himself much thinner...

He sneaks around the circle and waits upon the wind,
To blow real hard so he escapes and they start to play again...
He likes to make himself real big to scare the other ones,
He turns into a dragon cause he thinks it's lots of fun...

The smaller ones love Tuffy, he plays with them all day,
Until the sun shines very bright and makes them go away,
All the clouds must take the time, to sleep and grow up strong,
Then they'll be back another day, it won't be very long...

Written by: Nancy E. Hutcherson
November 3, 2001

*** *Tuffy The Cloud III* ***

The morning started sunny then the clouds came rolling in,
Now is the time for Tuffy to start his day again...
He showed up as a little horse, prancing very high,
Then he changed into a bird, oh how he could fly...

Today he was so happy, he had lots of things to do,
He had rested for a long, long while and now he felt brand new...
The bird that Tuffy had become, was starting to change its form,
He turned into a circus clown holding a funny horn...

He stayed like that for not too long for the others were coming fast,
He had to move quite quickly so there wouldn't be a crash...
When the clouds all get together, they make different sizes and
shapes,
They float and then they catch the wind, as though they cannot
wait...

But something now was happening, the big clouds turned dark gray,
Time now for Tuffy and his friends to work and not to play...
The rain was building up inside of each and every cloud,
The wind blew hard, the lightning struck, they knew the storm was
now...

Now you could not see Tuffy or his other little friends,
Because it now was raining hard, their work now just begins...
They have to make the thunder so the lightning can display,
And the flowers, plants and all the trees get their water on this day...

And now the storm is leaving and the sun is shining through,
Little white clouds are back playing, there's no more work to do...
Be sure that you watch Tuffy and his little friends each day,
Enjoy the things that they become, just pretend and you can play...

Written by: Nancy E. Hutcherson
November 3, 2001

Katie
Goes into
The
Attic

By

Nancy E. Hutcherson

*** *The Attic* ***

Katie crept up the attic stairs to see what treasures were
there,
She always wanted to do it so she took her brother's dare…
She opened the door at the top of the stairs and slowly went
into the room,
It was hard to see because the place was filled with dark and
gloom…

She stood real still while her eyes adjusted to the light that
was hardly there,
She heard a noise behind an old trunk, she felt a little
scared…
But Katie loved adventure and this was her cup of tea,
She would never tell her brothers what was there and what
she would see…

Quietly she opened an old trunk, it had blankets, books and a
hat,
She took them out one by one as on the floor she sat…
She opened a box that held pictures that were worn, faded
and old,
She shivered as she viewed them, she was starting to feel
cold…

She didn't know the people though one looked like her dad,
It was a little blonde headed boy and he seemed like he was
sad…
She wished that she knew the people especially the little boy,
She thought she could make him happy if she gave him her
brother's toy…

She heard her brothers calling from the bottom of the stairs,
They asked what she was doing and what she found up
there...
She wasn't going to tell them for they dared her to go in,

She put the things back in the trunk and closed the lid and
then...
She called out, you won't believe, the things I see up here,
Then laughed a little to herself knowing they wouldn't come
near...

Opening the door and descending the stairs she was thinking
of what she would say...
Wanting to scare her brothers, she started running away...

They quickly followed behind her wanting to know what was
there,
She stopped when she entered the kitchen and acted like she
was scared...
She said, I'll never go back there, there are things too scary to
say,
But she planned her return to the attic, she would go the very
next day...

Written by: Nancy E. Hutcherson
November 6, 2001

The Attic – Next Day

Katie got up early, her family asleep in the house,
She tiptoed past her brother's room being quiet as a mouse…
She was going back to the attic to see what she could find,
Another day in the attic, this morning she had lots of time…

As she opened the door, slowly, the morning sun streaming in,
So excited she could hardly wait, her adventure would now
begin…
Today was the day for boxes, there were 3 in the corner
alone,
Opening the lid of the first one, she took out an old telephone..

Katie knew that this was a treasure, the handle was ivory &
gold,
There weren't any buttons to push on, she knew it had to be
old…
The numbers were in a circle, it was hard to turn them around,
It was really very pretty, this old telephone she had found…

It must have belonged to a Princess, it was much too fancy for
a man,
The lady had to be lovely, who held this phone in her hand…
Katie could really imagine, how life must have been in those
days,
Pretty dresses and lots of tea parties, oh what a fun time to
play…

Just then she heard her mother, calling from the kitchen
below,
Her adventure for now was over, and she knew that she had
to go…
But she would come back later, there were so many things to
see,
This was her own place in the attic, she knew it would always
be…

Written by: Nancy E. Hutcherson, November 10, 2001

The Attic – III

Her brothers were outside playing and her mother was
washing her hair,
Now was the time for Katie's adventure back upstairs…
She felt quit good in the attic, it wasn't a scary room,
Even though she told her brothers, it was full of dark and
gloom…

She was ready to open the boxes, there were two that she
had not seen,
She was anxious to get them open, it was almost like a
dream…
The first one held a tea set, Katie couldn't believe her eyes,
There was a teapot with cups and saucers, oh what a nice
surprise…

She took them out very gently and placed them on the floor,
She needed someone to share with, that's what tea parties
are for…
Removing some tissue paper from something that felt like
glass,
Katie's mouth suddenly opened and she let out a gasp…

In her arms she held a dolly, the most beautiful she'd ever
seen,
With long red hair and big green eyes and her skin was
smooth as cream…
The dress that she wore was lovely though it seemed a little
worn,
And her hat and gloves were faded and her cape had been
torn…

But this didn't bother Katie for her tea party would begin,
They could laugh and chat and sip their tea while becoming
very best friends…
She decided to name the doll Scarlet, it was such a beautiful
name,

And everything was going quite nicely with Katie's make
believe game...

The afternoon was going fast, it was time for Katie to go,
She replaced the tea set in the box so no one would ever
know...
Wrapping Scarlet in the tissue, Katie knew that she'd be
missed,
But she would return another day and she blew Miss Scarlet a
kiss...

Written by: Nancy E. Hutcherson
November 11, 2001

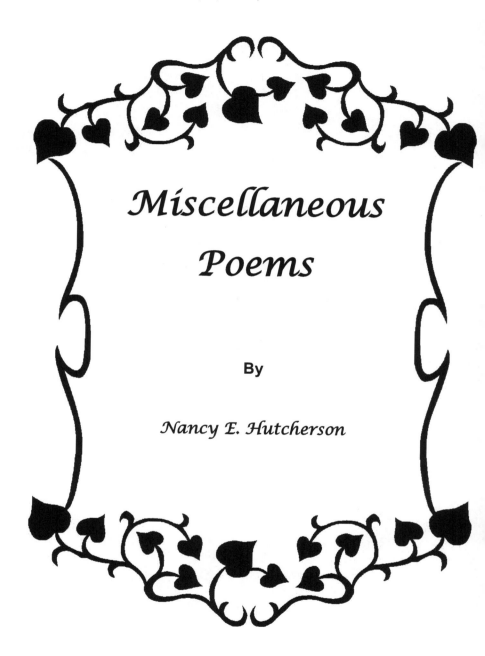

Miscellaneous Poems

By

Nancy E. Hutcherson

Poetry by Nancy E. Hutcherson
Duke Dog Saves Miss Chewy

It was way back in the winter, about 6 years ago,
Miss Chewy, our kitty cat went out into the snow…
She would come back in the evenings, to sleep where it was warm,
But this time she did not return, we didn't know where she had gone.

Two days past, it was at night, and John told Duke the dog,
You must go find Miss Chewy and bring her back to all…
Early the next morning when he started out to work,
He saw Duke lying in the yard with Chewy, she was hurt…

He ran outside and brought her in all muddy cold and scared,
She had been shot, 2 broken legs and blood all in her hair…
It broke my heart to see her, I held her cold and wet,
We wanted so to save her so John took her to the vet…

You see our Duke Dog found her and drug her till she dropped,
Her collar broke there in the yard and that's where Duke Dog
stopped…
She could not make her way back home, for there were hills to
climb,
So Duke Dog went to find her and saved her just in time…

The doctor set her broken legs and we prayed that they would heal,
He said no more could she go out and roam upon the hills…
You really need to see her, our Chewy is well and strong,
She ventures out into the yard, but she's not gone for long…

Now I am here to tell you, this story is sad but true,
It makes you wonder why people do the things they do…
Why would someone shoot a pet that has a collar on,
Knowing that she has a home and to others she belongs…

Written by: Nancy E. Hutcherson
November 11, 2001

Knock on Heaven's Door

Twice I've knocked on Heaven's door,
And twice been turned away...
My Lord told me, "It's not your time,"
You have a lot more days...

I asked Him why I'd come so close,
To entering Heaven's gate...
He said, "My child I've plans for you,
Be patient and just wait"...

An angel came and took my hand,
She guided me back to life...
She said, "You have a husband,
And he still needs his wife"...

You also have a daughter,
A mother, grandchildren too...
The Father up in Heaven,
Has things for you to do...

You'll live your life upon this earth,
Until your time has come...
And that will only be when,
The Lord's will has been done...

Don't question why He does the things,
That you don't understand...
Just know how much He loves you,
You're in His master plan...

Written by: Nancy E. Hutcherson
February 10, 2002

Deep Dark Hole

I feel as if I'm in a hole so dark I want to shout,
I cannot see an opening and I never will get out...
These feelings are so real to me, they will never go away,
I just cannot imagine ever seeing a sunny day...

Depression is an evil thing that comes upon my soul,
It takes my hopes, my dreams away and keeps me in this hole...
I cry, I scream, I beat my head, at God I start to shout,
Why have you put me in this hole, why won't you get me out...

I always take the medicine that is supposed to make me cope,
It usually works but times like this, I feel I have no hope...
My critters, friends and family don't seem to help a bit,
They say I shouldn't feel this way, that doesn't make me quit...

I know I'm not the only one, so often I've been told,
Not even that can help me when I'm way down in this hole...
My family and my friends tell me, I should not feel this way,
That God has been so good to me, I only need to pray...

I'M well aware that God loves me and that He lives within,
And Jesus died upon the cross to take away my sins...
But somehow it just doesn't help, I'm hurting in my soul,
I cannot see the light above when I'm way down in this hole...

I feel as though I cannot live this life God gave to me,
I'm so depressed and nothing is the way that it should be...
But I just keep on hanging on, I've gotten out before,
Because He always walks with me and holds an open door...

If you are feeling down and out and want to give up and die,
Remember I've been there also, and I came out alive...
It's not an easy path to walk but never are we alone,
He's with us every step of the way, He will always bring us home...

Written by: Nancy E. Hutcherson – October, 2001

*** *My Home* ***

When people ask me how I came to live in such a place,
I tell them of the story and goodness of God's grace...
It sounds as though I made it up, but that just isn't true,
It all really happened, everything I'm telling you...

My Lord above gave me this home even though I could not see,
His plans were better than mine were, He is so good to me...
I didn't want to live out here, I thought I was too good,
It wasn't where the happenings were, it was way out in the woods...

I thought that I could trick the Lord and with a little luck,
The sellers would not sell to us, they did and I was stuck...
I had a conversation with the Lord above that night,
I asked Him why I must be here, the area wasn't right...

But He just listened to my complaints, the way He always does,
And started changes in my heart, and filled me up with love...
It really wasn't simple, I fought Him all the way,
I didn't like the people and I didn't want to stay...

But as the house was being built I started to believe,
That God knows best and this is where, He wanted me to be...
Everything is beautiful, my home, the trees the view,
My husband, church and critters, He gave these to me too...

I know someday I'll leave this place to whom God brings along,
And they will love it like I do, for God is never wrong...
So if you want a home like mine, just trust it to the Lord,
And He will always guide the way, of this I'm very sure...

Written by: Nancy E. Hutcherson
October, 2001

*** First Frost ***

The first frost came and I went out to see,
My flowers frozen and dead...
But to my surprise, they were all alive,
Still standing tall in the beds...

How could this be with 23 degrees,
Being the temperature for the night...
My Lord above surely showed me love,
What a wonderful glorious sight...

The frost was on the windshield,
So I know how cold it was...
But my flowers were protected,
With God's warm tender love...

I talk to my Lord, every day,
For that's how I get through...
And He always answers in different ways,
And He shows me what I should do...

We all have troubles in our lives,
Fear not for God is there...
He's waiting for a word from you,
To show how much He cares...

Written by: Nancy E. Hutcherson
October 30, 2001

*** The Cold, The Dark, The Wind ***

The night is dark, it's cold outside, the wind is blowing strong,
I pray this feeling that I have, does not last very long...
I sit here in my easy chair and think of brighter days,
When life was much more simple with lots of time for play...

My grandma used to say to me, don't wish your life away,
You will be grown, before you know, better listen to what I say...
But I would wish and wish and wish to get into my teens,
I didn't really understand what growing up would mean...

But life is so much different now, with terror going on,
You cannot open a letter without wondering if something's wrong...
You don't want your kids to go out and play for fear they'll come to
harm,
You want to keep them close to you and hold them in your arms...

This isn't how God planned our lives, it was love we were to have,
But as each century came along, we changed till things got bad...
It's up to us to change it now and refuse to let evil win,
We must ask God to guide us now and forgive us all our sins...

To put God back upon His Throne and praise Him every day,
To love each other as we should, this is the only way...
For then we do not have to fear the dark, the cold, the wind,
For He will take all that away and we'll be His children again...

Written by: Nancy E. Hutcherson
October, 2001

*** *Feed The Birds* ***

Yellow, orange, green and red, the colors of the leaves,
Floating here and landing there, they leave the barren trees...
Fall is here and summer's gone, these leaves soon will be dead,
They'll cover every inch of ground as a comforter on a bed...

The naked trees stand cold and tall swaying with the breeze,
As if to say, there's nothing more until we plant our seeds...
The birds are landing on the limbs, surveying all the ground,
Singing to each other, there's no food there to be found...

God has blessed me with this home, high upon this hill,
There's not much land around here left, for houses it does fill...
The birds and all the creatures, depend on us for food,
I will surely do my part, I hope that you will too...

God gave to us these creatures, to care for them each day,
He never meant for man to take their trees and land away...
For if we do, we must take care of each and every thing,
For if we don't when spring time comes, there'll be no birds to sing..

Be sure to fill your feeders, with a variety of seeds,
So all the birds around your home will have the food they need...
For once you start to feed them, never can you quit,
You see they must depend on us, for every single bit...

Written by: Nancy E. Hutcherson
October, 2001

*** *The Hummingbirds* ***

I put out a feeder for the hummingbirds to feed,
I wait in anticipation for the first one that I see…
It's spring time now and time for them, to scout out and to find,
The nectar of the flowers and these feeders that are mine…

It is quite amusing to watch them guard their food,
They do not wish to share at all, they're really very rude…
A new one comes upon the scene and wants a little sip,
The old one says, there's not a chance and gives a little hit…

They fly around like bombers protecting what is theirs,
They do not want another one, flying in their air…
I really don't believe that they are bad as what they seem,
They may just be pretending and acting very mean.

I came upon the deck one day and heard a humming sound,
It was coming from the trash can by the door upon the ground…
I picked it up and looked inside and much to my surprise,
A precious little hummingbird was stuck way down inside…

It was trying to find something, to gather for its nest,
To cushion all the babies and have a place to rest…
And in the can was dog hair that I got from brushing Bear,
The little hummingbird got caught in all the long dog hair…

I reached into the trash can and gently took her out,
She was such a small thing and so scared there was no doubt…
I took the hair off of her head and pulled it from her wings,
She seemed to know I would not hurt this tiny, little thing…

She had a few hairs in her mouth then took off like a flash,
I said a prayer, she'd be OK, she never did look back…
It felt so good to know that I had helped this little one,
I do enjoy these hummingbirds, watching them is fun…

Written by: Nancy E. Hutcherson, October 31, 2001

*** *These Little Seeds of Mine* ***

I was walking in the woods enjoying nature's land,
I found some seeds upon the ground and held them in my hand...
I didn't know what kind they were or even of their worth,
But I took them home, dug a hole, and covered them with earth...

I watered and I fed them and the sun shown bright for weeks,
And then one day they started to sprout, it gave me such a treat...
I watered, fed and gave them food and watched them as they grew,
I didn't have an inkling of what they'd turn in to...

As time went on the bright green leaves, appeared upon a vine,
They started climbing up the tree, these little seeds of mine...
Some blooms appeared, their color was a rich and lovely red,
It was a glorious thing to see, these flowering in the bed...

I still did not know what they were, just lying there alone,
These little seeds upon the ground I picked up and brought home...
Their foliage was so beautiful as the blooms began to die,
And in their place a pod appeared and I did not know why.

I watched them as the days grew cool and the season turned to fall,
These pods grew dark upon the vine, some large and some were
small...
And then the frost came to the yard and the vine was on the ground,
Out popped the seeds, just like the ones in the woods that I had
found.

I still do not know what they are but it matters not to me,
For I enjoyed the leaves, the blooms & the pods that gave me
seeds...
Next spring, I shall plant them, in my yard and all around,
These little seeds that God gave me, I found them on the ground...

Written by: Nancy E. Hutcherson
October 31, 2001

*** *CRITTER HEAVEN* ***

We all know there's a heaven where God and angels live,
With homes someday for everyone who choose God's way to live...
But do you know there's a heaven for critters of every kind,
For when they die, that's where they go, your pets and also mine...

I lost my cat, The General, He died 3 years ago,
He was one of many pets that live in our household...
It hurt the day we lost him for he slept upon our bed,
We had our evening ritual and now my friend was dead...

We buried him in the back yard between 2 big oak trees,
He'll always be here with us because his grave I see...
But really he's in heaven with other critters too,
When life on earth has ended, there's a better place to choose...

So if you lose a pet of yours, try not to grieve for long,
Just know that they're in heaven with God where they belong...
And someday we will see them up in these heavenly places,
Playing like they did while here, with smiles upon their faces...

Written by: Nancy E. Hutcherson
November 19, 2001

*** THE SPARROW ***

I was feeling sad and lonely and talking to my Lord,
I had a real bad problem, one that I could not ignore...
I was listening to Christian music and a song I love to hear,
His Eye is On The Sparrow was sounding in my ears...

A bird flew at the window, it thought it still was air,
I ran outside and picked it up, my cat knew it was there...
I looked, it was a sparrow lying in my hand,
God was telling me that He heard and understands...

I didn't want the sparrow to lose its life that day,
And so I asked my God above to let it fly away...
I know you won't believe it but I promise this is true,
That sparrow's life was over but he sat up and he flew...

Some people ask me how I know that God is true and real,
I tell them of this story, and just what I really feel...
He'll show you if you ask Him, that is all you have to do...
For His eye is on the sparrow, oh how much more He cares for you.

Written by: Nancy E. Hutcherson
October, 2001

Poetry by Nancy E. Hutcherson
The Knock on the Door

Back in the early 70's my life was a total mess,
Divorced and raising a little girl, as a mother I wasn't the best...
I felt so alone and worthless, my self-esteem wasn't there,
I cried all the time when I was at home cause I felt that nobody
cared...

Why should anyone care for me, I failed at all I did,
I got so low, I just wanted to sleep and I really didn't want to live...
There were times I acted self-assured so people would not see,
What a miserable person I really was, cause happiness wasn't for
me...

Then one day while Deb was at school, there came a knock on my
door,
A woman selling children's books, I thought to myself, what for...
I really wanted her to leave so I bought the books that day,
And as she was leaving, she gave me her card as she spoke in a very
nice way...

There is a pastor new to town who is teaching not far from here,
I'd love to take you with me sometime, she sounded so very
sincere...
I thanked her as I closed the door, knowing I'd never go,
God didn't have any use for me, that much I did know...

The months went by, I lived my life as though I was in a trance,
I took my pills and drank a lot and then go out and dance...
My life grew more unbearable, I had to stop the pain,
Nothing seemed to help me, I thought I'd go insane...

And then one day I found her card among the books I bought,
I took the phone and called her up, not knowing where to start...
I said I'd like to go with her to hear this pastor teach,
I don't know why I did that, God was out of my reach...

I walked into this living room with women all around,
I wanted to scream, I don't belong here, but I didn't make a sound...
When the Pastor started teaching I knew he spoke to me,
The tears were swelling in my eyes so much I could not see...

I left when it was over, vowed never to return,
I wasn't good like those women and I didn't know how to learn...
I did go back one more time and the same thing happened again,
I know now it was Satan trying to keep me in my sin.

But something started happening when the tears came like before,
The Pastor came up to me and he stopped me at the door...
He said, I hope you call me if you ever find the need,
I thanked him and I left that day, no more of me he'd see...

I tried so hard to change my ways and live a better life,
But what on earth was there for me, I was no longer a wife...
I had this little girl of mine who needs a father too,
I felt so very useless, I didn't know what to do...

One morning I made her lunch and sent her off to school,
I couldn't stand this pain anymore, I knew what I must do...
I opened up my bureau and slowly took out my gun,
I was crying hard and shaking but I knew what must be done...

While sitting on the bedside, I cried out to The Lord,
I fell down on my knees and cried until my throat was sore...
I prayed Dear God, if you are here and have a better way,
Please stop me for I hurt so bad, I cannot live this way...

Then at that very moment there was a knock upon my door,
I thought it was my sister like so many times before...
I laid the gun down on the bed and quietly looked out,
And when I saw who was standing there, I knew there was no
doubt...

This man was dressed in blue jeans with a Bible in his hand,

It was that same young pastor, I could not understand...

Did God really send him to my home upon this day,
Did God really love me and did He have a better way...

I asked this Pastor to come in, I was shaking with such fear,
I couldn't believe God answered but why else was he here...
We sat down at the table and he spoke so soft and low,
The Holy Spirit told him to come so he knew he had to go...

He was working in his garden and trimming up the grass,
But he stopped and told his wife to call the woman in the class...
And find out what my name was and how to get to me,
For the Holy Spirit told him, he knew I was in need...

I was listening as he told me God made me the way I am,
He wanted only good for me and I needed to understand,
When Jesus died upon that cross, he died also for me,
If He could love me that much then who was I not to believe...

That day will always be with me, for that was when I knew,
God made me the way I am, just like He made you too...

My life still isn't perfect for there is no such a thing,
But that day I accepted Jesus Christ, my life is not the same...
I still have trials and problems but you must understand,
My Lord is always with me and I know He holds my hand...

Written by: Nancy E. Hutcherson
November 13, 2001

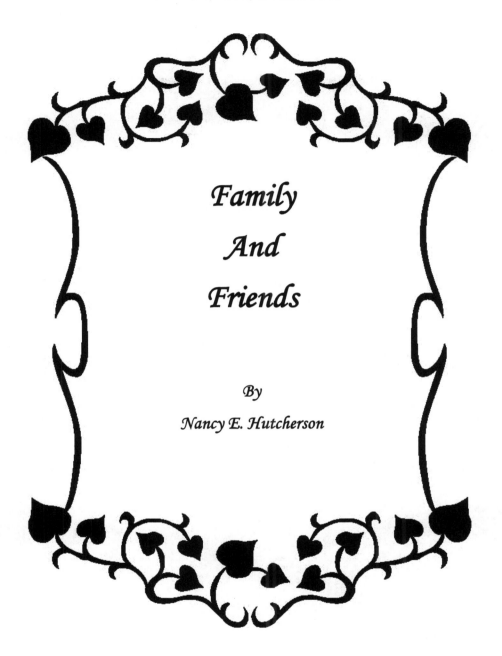

Family

And

Friends

By

Nancy E. Hutcherson

*** GOD'S GIFT ***

Baby Will is a precious child,
A gift from GOD to you...
He'll give you joy & happiness,
From now till your life's through...

There will be times when sorrow comes,
But GOD will hold your hand...
HE'LL give the strength to carry on,
No one can understand...

You and Scott will watch him grow,
And marvel at his charm...
You'll know he is the brightest child,
That's ever come along...

Enjoy these days you have right now,
They'll pass before you know...
Your son will be a man so soon,
You'll wonder where time goes...

Always know I'm here for you,
Although we're miles away...
I love you and your family,
Much more than I can say...

You'll always be my baby Jen,
As long as I'm alive...
And Will shall be your baby boy,
On that you can rely...

May of 2001
Written by: Aunt Nancy Hutcherson

Poetry by Nancy E. Hutcherson
YOUR MOM IS NOW IN HEAVEN

This isn't meant to make you cry,
Or shed a single tear...
It's only meant to let you know,
Our Father's always here...

Your mom is on a journey,
Where her angels all abide...
She has entered the Kingdom,
With Jesus by her side...

While here on earth, she did His will,
Of that we know is true...
She spread the Word, she gave her all,
She was faithful, strong & true...

When she got sick, I prayed to God,
That He would make her well...
I asked Him for a miracle.
I thought that I had failed...

And, then He gave you time with her,
And took her pain away...
The miracle I prayed for,
He gave to you that day...

And now that she's in heaven,
No more work on earth to do...
She is singing with the Angels,
And she's watching over you...

Dear Kerry, you are such a dear
Your faith will keep you strong...
Your mom is now in Heaven,
With The Lord, where she belongs...

By: Nancy Hutcherson
Inspired by God August 8, 2001

HAPPY BIRTHDAY
****MOTHER****

Mother dearest it's a wonderful day,
84 years on this earth you've stayed...

You had two girls of whom you're proud,
One is perfect the other LOUD!

You did the best that you could do,
Arlene's like daddy and I'm just like you...

You came out good on the grandchildren you had,
3 were good and 1 kinda bad...
She was like me, a little wild,
But she turned around and made us proud...

Now your great grandchildren are a sight to behold,
You have so many, they are making us old...
First came Nick & then came John next was Drew
Then Alex came along...

Ethan was next, then Maddie arrived and Addison showed up,
With big brown eyes...
Katie was the baby till February Twenty-eight,
When Will arrived for his big date...

When you were young did you believe,
You'd live this long and get to see...
9 great grandchildren with brown eyes and blue,

Happy Birthday Mother (Mamaw)
We all love you,

ARLENE & DON   NANCY & JOHN
SCOTT & KAREN   DEBORAH & WILL
ALEX, ETHAN & ADDISON   NICK, JOHN & KATIE
SHARON & BILLY
DREW & MADDIE
JENNIFER & SCOTT
WILL

Written by: Nancy E. Hutcherson
March 4, 2001

A MIRACLE WAS BORN

On May 24th, Two thousand and one,
At 8:05 P.M...
Baby Sam Corum came into this world,
Hi family just waiting for him...

Shari and Larry, your life won't be the same,
From now until he is grown...
You will laugh and you'll cry over things that he does,
But never will you be alone...

The Lord above has Sam in His hands,
And his guardian Angel will stay...
Close to you child all of his life,
You two need only to pray...

Enjoy

Written by: Nancy E. Hutcherson

SISTERS

God made us to be sisters
He knows what's best to do.....
And even though we're different
Our sameness still shows through....

You're loving and you're giving
You care for everyone....
Your prayers brought me through hard times
I'm glad those years are done....

I love you, you're my sister
I know you love me too....
I am here should you need me
You've always seen me through....

Though both our lives are different
We travel separate roads....
We'll end up at the same place
Our Heavenly Father knows....

Written by: Nancy E. Hutcherson
December 18, 2005

MOTHER

I know it wasn't easy,
Raising a girl like me…
Always in to everything,
And wanting everything I'd see…

But you always had patience,
And showed me right from wrong…
And helped me with my homework,
When your work days were so long…

When I was in high school,
You would sew my party gowns…
The most beautiful ones I'd ever seen,
Not a prettier one could be found…

And then when I got married,
And became a mother too…
I understood just why you did,
The things you'd always do…

I'm thanking you dear mother,
For giving all your love…
There's never been a better Mom,
I say this with all my love…

I love YOU Mom!

Written by: Nancy E. Hutcherson
December 2, 2001

*** MOTHERS ***

Thank you for all you've done,
To help me become a man...
You always listen to me,
And said you understand...

You showed me what's important,
In life and how to live...
You gave me independence,
And taught me how to give...

You never put me down at all,
Or made me feel ashamed...
If I didn't always win,
When playing baseball games...

Though times I did not show it,
But I hope you always knew...
I'm very proud to be your son,

Dear Mother
I
Love You

Written by: Nancy E. Hutcherson
December 2, 2001

*** Dear Heavenly Father ***

Please bless this earthly home,
And all who dwell within...
Guard them from the evil one,
The one we know as sin...

Let them know that YOU are here,
In daytime and at night...
And Your angels will protect them,
For they're always in Your sight...

Let them feel your presence,
In everything they do...
And know their biggest problem,
Is never too big for YOU...

Thank You Heavenly Father,
For listening to my prayer...
And caring for Your children,
And for always being there...

Written by: Nancy E. Hutcherson
January, 2002

*** *GIRL FRIENDS* ***

We met in 1988,
I'll never forget that day…
I looked at you, you looked at me,
There was really nothing to say…

We didn't like each other,
That much we both knew…
But God had different plans for us,
And so our friendship grew…

His timing was so perfect,
For we both needed a friend…
We walked, we talked, we laugh a lot,
On each other we would depend…

You moved away, off of the hill,
You needed a brand new start…
Now we don't see each other much,
But you're still in my heart…

I love you like a sister,
You've never let me down…
And when you ever need me,
You know I'll be around…

Our lives are both so different,
But true friendship never fades…
We can call upon each other,
Until our dying days…

Written by: Nancy E. Hutcherson
December 24, 2001

FRIENDS

Lord, bless this home and those within,
That live for You each day...
Give them joy and peace and hope,
And always light their way...

Friends are worth much more than gold,
These two, You've given me...
They've showed me just how much they care,
In good times and in need...

They truly care and show Your love,
In all they say and do...
And anyone that meets them,
Knows that this is true...

I lift them up to you right now,
Please let them know I care...
I'll always be a friend to them,
Our love for You, we share...

Written by: Nancy E. Hutcherson
February, 2002

FRIENDS

You are a special friend to me
You know that this true…
I love you like a sister
No matter what you do…

I know that you are here for me
In sorrow and in pain…
And I am also here for you
My feelings are the same…

So let's be happy in this life
That God has given free…
We share our joys and sorrows
You mean so much to me…

Written by: Nancy E. Hutcherson
Inspired by God
December, 2005

Katherine Elizabeth Hailey Hightower

In early 1917 she came into this world,
Born to James and Elizabeth was a tiny baby girl…

Her early life she grew into a beautiful loving teen,
She met our dad and married him when she was just 18…

The depression wasn't an easy time for her and for our dad,
But she was always grateful for everything she had…

Age 20 she gave birth to her precious baby girl,
She gave the name Arlene, the most beautiful in the world…

Age 25 another girl came into their lives,
Arlene named me Nancy and no one knows just why…

As time went on she worked hard, days and night times too…
We never really appreciated all the things she'd do…

She made our evening dresses when her work day was done,
The most beautiful at the parties, we were proud of every one…

We grew up and then we married, her grandchildren were her joy,
3 lovely girls she loved so much and 1 very handsome boy…

Time moved on, she never stopped giving love to others,
No one in this whole, wide world could have a better mother…
This hasn't done you justice, there's so much more to say,
But you know what is in our hearts, today and every day…

So thank you Mom for all you did, you were the best no doubt,
We'll miss you but our memories never will run out…

Written by: Nancy E. Hutcherson
January 14, 2007

*** Mary Katherine Davis ***

Today is Katie's birthday, she's just turned 2 years old,
She has a mind that is her own and her heart is pure as gold...
Her big blue eyes and light blonde hair are traits she gets from dad,
Her mother's traits come out in her when sometimes she acts bad...

She follows both her brothers till they turn and yell at her,
You cannot come with us Miss Kate, you're just a little girl...
Big ole tears form in her eyes and then she starts to cry,
She yells and screams and kicks her feet, you'd think she's gonna die...

John reaches down and squeezed her so she will stop the fuss,
Nick turns around and yells at John, she's still not coming with us...
She loves her brothers very much, she wants to be with them,
But they just want to go outside, and play with all their friends...

Then mommy comes into the room to love her tears away,
So Nick and John can go outside and have their time to play...
But Katie's wanting none of that, she's determined to win the fight,
She reminds me of her mother when I would put her to bed at night...

The front door now is opened and her daddy's coming in,
She stops her tears, her screams, her cries, she's running up to him...
He picks her up and says what's wrong, giving her a little twirl,
Now everything's forgotten, for she is her daddy's girl...

Written by: Nancy E. Hutcherson
(Granmaw) October 21, 2001

Mary Katherine Davis

Born October 21, 1999

The day she came into this world was such a sight to see,
Big blue eyes, and not much hair, my Katie came to me…

Her smile and laugh were Heaven sent we knew she was our own,
This small, precious baby girl that came into our home…

Her brothers laughed with lots of joy, a sister in their lives,
They thought that it was lots of fun seeing twinkles in her eyes…

It meant the world to me to have this precious little girl,
A granddaughter to hug and love and teach about this world…

Her will is strong, she tries her best to get her every way,
But she has learned that she must do what grandma has to say…

Katie means the world to me, she reminds me of her Mother,
She tries her best to wear me down just like her two big brothers…

She is an angel, heaven sent, I thank the Lord above,
He gave us Katie Davis and wrapped her up in love…

Written by: Nancy E. Hutcherson, grandmother
September 29, 2005

Poetry

At Christmas

Written by

Nancy E. Hutcherson

MERRY CHRISTMAS

You are the main man in my life,
And such a great dad too...
But how come is it 20 bucks,
Is all you have with you...

And tell me please, what's with your mind,
The F word's all you say...
It's I forget or I forgot,
It's the same thing every day...

So here's some money just for you,
To keep so you won't holler...
The next time you stop at the store,
You'll have more than 20 dollars...

As for your memory to help you out,
I have some purple string...
To tie around your finger,
Right next to your wedding ring...

And

HAPPY NEW YEAR

Written by: Nancy E. Hutcherson
2001

MERRY CHRISTMAS

You're a biker and you ride a Harley,
That's a truth that everyone knows...
But Bikers are such different people,
If you ride one you must play the roll...

They dress in their leather jackets,
And leather boots on their feet...
They always have their honey,
Sitting behind on their seat...

There is one more thing that they wear,
So I thought I would get it for you...
It goes around your forehead,
And I got you one that's brand new...

I was told they call it a DO RAG,
All bikers say that it's neat...
So I wanted you to have one,
So your outfit would be complete...

AND

HAPPY NEW YEAR

Written by: Nancy E. Hutcherson
2001

WHY CHRISTMAS

The birth was known to all around,
Three Wise men came to see...
The baby born in Bethlehem,
With gifts they brought to Thee...

The Shepherds tending flocks of sheep,
They saw the star that night...
The Angels came to give the news,
The meaning of the light...

Twas baby Jesus that they seeked,
He came to knock at our door...
To save us from the evil one,
And give us hope once more...

We've all been told throughout His word,
How much He cares for us...
The only thing we have to do,
Is give Him all our trust...

Even if you don't believe,
This story that is true...
Please answer the door and let Him in,
What Do You Have To Lose?????

Written by: God
Typed by: Nancy E. Hutcherson
December 23, 2001

HAPPY BIRTHDAY JESUS

Happy birthday Jesus,
I'm so glad that you came...
To this earth in human form,
To take away our pain...

It tells us in the Bible,
That there would come a Lamb...
Born of the Virgin Mary,
Somewhere in Bethlehem...

And sure enough as it was told,
You were born upon that night...
Three wise men followed the star above,
That shined so very bright...

They brought you gifts,
So rare and fine...
For an angel told them so,
That You were sent from God above...
To let the whole world know...

How much He truly cares for us,
He wants for us the best...
We only have to ask Him,
And He will do the rest...

So on Your birthday, Jesus,
We take this time to say...
Thank you for Your sacrifice,
And showing us the way...

HAPPY BIRTHDAY, JESUS!

Written by: GOD
Typed by: Nancy E. Hutcherson 2001

My husband John with Shasta

Shasta

This is where Shasta sleeps – with me

My daughter Deborah and granddaughter Katie

Shasta

Fountain for birds, squirrels, critters and dogs for watering. A lot of fun watching them in the fountain especially the birds and squirrels taking a bath.

When I'm in the bed I can see my bird feeders and this is the squirrel that steals the seeds. I don't mind I really love watching him.

KEYTA with her Always ball

Jillian in her special place where she can guard the house
and keep unwanted dogs away.

Keyta on the deck waiting for someone to play ball.

This is Katie, my granddaughter. I wrote The Attic for her. She is now 15, goes to the Nashville School of Arts and plays the Violin with the Williamson County orchestra.

My friend, Sue Hamilton's Theo

My friend, Sue Hamilton's Theo

Poetry by Nancy E. Hutcherson

ISBN-13:978-1511736350

ISBN-10:1511736356

Heart of My Heart Publishing Co., LLC

www.three-sheep.com

Made in the USA
San Bernardino, CA
19 May 2015